THE FAST WAY T
BEST MAN'S SPEECH

BULLET GUIDE

Matt Avery

Hodder Education, 338 Euston Road, London NW1 3BH

Hodder Education is an Hachette UK company

First published in UK 2011 by Hodder Education

This edition published 2011

Artworks (internal and cover): Peter Lubach
Cover concept design: Two Associates

British Library Cataloguing in Publication Data: a catalogue record for this title is available from the British Library.

10 9 8 7 6 5 4 3 2 1

The publisher has used its best endeavours to ensure that any website addresses referred to in this book are correct and active at the time of going to press. However, the publisher and the author have no responsibility for the websites and can make no guarantee that a site will remain live or that the content will remain relevant, decent or appropriate.

The publisher has made every effort to mark as such all words which it believes to be trademarks. The publisher should also like to make it clear that the presence of a word in the book, whether marked or unmarked, in no way affects its legal status as a trademark.

Every reasonable effort has been made by the publisher to trace the copyright holders of material in this book. Any errors or omissions should be notified in writing to the publisher, who will endeavour to rectify the situation for any reprints and future editions.

Hachette UK's policy is to use papers that are natural, renewable and recyclable products and made from wood grown in sustainable forests. The logging and manufacturing processes are expected to conform to the environmental regulations of the country of origin.

www.hoddereducation.co.uk

Typeset by Stephen Rowling/Springworks

Printed in Spain

To Rich

Acknowledgements

My sincere thanks to everyone who contributed to this book with details of their experiences; and to those whose support made it possible, especially my family, Victoria at Hodder Education, and Suze.

About the author

Matt Avery trained as an actor and speech and drama practitioner and has spent the last 20 years training people in public speaking for all manner of occasions, private and corporate, as well as practising what he preaches at his own wedding – and other people's!

In addition to lecturing in motivational speaking, Matt runs group coaching sessions for anyone who will be a speaker at a forthcoming wedding and who would like some expert guidance.

Please visit perfectweddingspeechesfast.com for more information.

Contents

Introduction

'There are only two types of speakers in the world – 1. The nervous and 2. Liars.'

Mark Twain

The happy couple's wedding day is without doubt one of the biggest days in their lives, and a key component is the speech everyone looks forward to the most – **the best man's speech.** So, like it or not, the pressure's on.

To enjoy the day to the full, and be able to concentrate on supporting the groom, you will need to be **completely confident** in your ability to give an entertaining and memorable speech when the time comes. Unfortunately, many best men find that the looming dread of having to stand up in front of the assembled audience of family and friends to give their speech completely overshadows the day.

Like many best men before you, you are bound to be feeling the pressure of having to get your speech just right. At a time when you should be enjoying the wonderful occasion to the full, worrying about giving your speech means you could miss out on the excitement of the build-up, the ceremony and the wedding breakfast.

Shouldn't you be able to enjoy giving your speech rather than just trying to get through it with your dignity intact and your lunch still in your stomach? What if it was something **you actually looked forward to doing**?

By **preparing thoroughly** – fully understanding what's involved and how you are likely to feel on the day, writing your speech carefully and perfecting its delivery, learning how to control your nerves (and even use them to your advantage) and getting your audience relaxed and on your side – you can turn giving your speech from something you endure into something you relish, a **highlight of your day** and a **cherished memory for the happy couple**.

This book shows you how.

1 Getting started early

Be prepared!

It may seem that the wedding is a long way off and that you have plenty of time, but **don't** be tempted into putting off preparing your speech. It will be remembered for a long time to come, especially by the bride and groom.

This is why it's worth **putting in the effort** to make it really good. Leaving it to the last minute or, worse still, just 'winging it' on the day is a recipe for disaster.

● Don't be tempted to put your feet up – the wedding will come round a lot faster than you think!

This chapter will help you **get organized**, and it tells you what you need to consider before you start writing your speech. It covers:

* the initial preparations you need to make
* your role on the day
* consulting and reassuring the bride and groom on the tone and content of your speech
* how to do research
* the first six things to do right now
* when you will need to give your speech
* the people you will have to thank and toast.

Don't put off preparing your speech

Initial preparations

When it comes to your wedding speech, there is no such thing as being over-prepared. Getting yourself **organized early** is important because it will help to:

* settle your nerves
* ensure that you **don't omit** anything important
* ensure that you **don't ad-lib** anything that you later regret
* give you the time and opportunity to **rehearse** your speech.

'Proper planning and preparation prevent poor performance.'

Charlie Batch

● Give yourself plenty of time to prepare your speech

4

Your role on the day

Your job on the day is primarily **to look after the groom** and ensure that he has whatever he needs, when he needs it.

In addition to giving your speech you'll be expected to:

* get the groom to the wedding venue **on time**
* **support** the groom throughout the day
* look after **the rings**
* **liaise** with the groom, the ushers and bridesmaids to make sure that everything **runs smoothly**
* ensure that the **photographer** has taken all the shots the bride and groom want
* act as **diplomat** and **peacemaker** if necessary!

You may also be asked to:

* call relevant people forward for the photos
* help the bride and groom to get away safely after the reception.

Consulting the bride and groom

The best man's speech can cause a degree of worry for the happy couple.

The groom may worry about:	The bride may worry about:
embarrassing or humiliating content	anecdotes about the groom's former girlfriends
unwanted revelations	a bawdy, 'lads' style of delivery
nasty surprises.	discomfort to the groom.

Consulting the bride and groom on your speech will:

* **reassure** them
* make them feel **included**
* avoid any regrets over **inclusions** or **omissions** to your speech.

How can I consult the bride and groom and still keep my speech a surprise?

Reassuring the bride and groom

The trick is to reassure the bride and groom about the tone and style of your speech while still managing to keep the contents a secret. The happy couple want to be surprised, but in a nice way.

Provided the bride and groom are reassured that your speech won't go 'too far', they will be able to enjoy it being a surprise on the day. Taking this **thoughtful** approach will show your support for the groom while earning you brownie points with the bride!

Reassure them that your speech …

will…

✔ be **appropriate**
✔ be **sensitive** in tone and style
✔ be **funny**

won't…

✗ cause **offence** to anyone
✗ mention **former girlfriends**
✗ be **lewd or bawdy** in nature.

The importance of research

You probably know the groom-to-be fairly well and have some shared experiences you can call upon for your speech, but **a little research** can provide **extra material** that will make it

* funnier
* more rounded
* **relevant** to as many guests as possible
* a **genuine surprise** for the bride and groom.

Remember
Doing a little careful research can also help you avoid upsetting anyone by saying the wrong thing.

If you don't know the groom-to-be well, your research will be even more vital. Consult his friends and family for information and any anecdotes.

'The best way to sound like you know what you're talking about is to know what you're talking about.'

Anon.

The six things to do right now

You can achieve the following six things right now. Achieving them will:

* help focus your mind on the task ahead
* prepare some necessary groundwork.

1 Begin sketching out a **draft plan** of your speech, however rough. This should be regularly updated.
2 **Consult the bride and groom** on your speech.
3 Speak to the groom's family and friends to **gather material** for your speech.
4 Know who is being invited – so that you can **pitch your speech appropriately.**
5 Start **practising** speaking out loud – and loudly – whenever you're on your own.
6 Line up some **willing volunteers** who can listen to you practise making your speech.

When to give your speech

Traditionally, there are **three wedding speeches.** They occur in this order:

1 father of the bride's speech
2 groom's speech
3 best man's speech.

So your speech will be **the last.** This is good because:

Remember
Your audience will already have sat through two speeches so you'll need to launch into your speech with **bundles of energy.**

* the other speakers will have **broken the ice** for you
* your audience will be nicely **warmed up**
* your speech is the one most people will be **most looking forward to** – so you'll get a great reception
* the groom is likely to have been very polite about you since your speech follows his!

Whom to thank and toast

It is traditional for the best man...

It's not traditional for the best man to present gifts.

* **to respond:**
    » to the groom's toast to the bridesmaids and pageboys
* **to read out:**
    » any telegrams or cards from family and friends unable to attend
* **to thank:**
    » the groom for choosing you as his best man
    » the bride and groom for their lovely gift
* **to compliment:**
    » the bride and the bridesmaids on how lovely they look
* **to propose a toast to:**
    » the health and happiness of the bride and groom.

Ask the bride and groom if they want to follow this traditional approach and sequence or whether they would prefer something different.

2 Writing your speech: the basics

The perfect wedding speech

You don't need to be a professional speech-writer to write the perfect wedding speech. To make it meaningful it needs to be **personal**. Cherry-picking material from sample speeches will only result in a bland speech that could be given by any best man about any groom, to any audience.

By **thinking about** what you want to say, **structuring** your thoughts carefully, and continually **improving** your speech as time goes by, you'll soon discover that everyone can write a great wedding speech.

● Think carefully about what you want to say…

This chapter explains the **key points** to consider when writing your speech. It tells you how to:

* start and finish strongly
* decide what to include
* structure your speech
* decide how long it should be
* set the tone
* meet audience expectations
* represent others
* personalize your speech.

Everyone can write a great wedding speech

Starting and finishing strongly

The **beginning** and **end** of your speech are the parts most likely to be **remembered**, so it is crucial to make sure that these are **really strong**.

A strong start will:	A strong finish will:
grab your audience's attention	bring your speech to a definite conclusion
help them relax (which will help you relax!)	leave on a high note
break the ice	leave the audience wanting more
make them want to listen to your speech.	round off the series of speeches.

Top tip
To get your speech off to a great start, a short anecdote or a (clean) joke will grab everyone's attention. A rousing toast is the traditional close.

What should you include?

Besides containing the **essential** thanks and toast (see chapter 1), the best man's speech is traditionally an opportunity to poke some **gentle** fun at the groom. How you do this largely depends on:

* how you want to come across
* how you think the groom and the guests will react.

However, the **golden rule** is to make sure your speech revolves around the groom. It's also important to remember that:

* your humour needs to be **appropriate**
* you should find time to **compliment the bride.**

If you're uncertain of quite how to pitch your speech, err on the side of **caution.** Your jokes should be funny but not humiliating or embarrassing.

'The secret of success is sincerity. Once you can fake that you've got it made.'
Jean Giraudoux

Structuring your speech

A good approach is to divide your speech into **sections** so that it takes your audience on a **journey**. For example:

1 Start with a short icebreaker joke to set the tone.

2 Tell the guests how long you've known the groom, and relate:
» some amusing anecdotes about him
» some of his milder misdemeanours.

3 As yours is the last speech, conclude with a final and resolute toast.

Top tip
Try to ensure that your speech flows from one section to the next.

Remember
Since your speech should be completely different in tone, style and content from the other two, begin with something punchy to differentiate it.

How long should it be?

The speeches are a part of the day to which most guests look forward. However, it is good to remember that:

A short speech…

✔ *will be more **memorable***
✔ *will leave the audience **wanting more***
✔ *might be a **pleasant surprise**!*

A long speech…

✘ *may make the audience **restless***
✘ *can appear **self-indulgent***
✘ *can easily become **boring**.*

Remember
Your audience will already have heard two speeches, and any audience has a maximum tolerance for listening. Less is more!

'Make sure you have finished speaking before your audience has finished listening.'

Dorothy Sarnoff

Setting the tone

Think of yourself in the same mould and with the same responsibilities as a **family-audience-friendly stand-up comedian.** The audience will not need to be told what to expect from your speech – they will be expecting it to be:

* funny
* gently ridiculing
* warm
* upbeat.

By setting an appropriate tone from the outset, you will get the audience relaxed and on your side and save yourself a lot of work. This can be achieved by:

Remember
The groom chose you as his best man because of your unique personality, so be yourself and let your speech reflect who you really are.

* starting with a strong joke
* being clear that you won't overstep the boundaries of good taste.

Audience expectations

Your audience will expect you to be **funny**, **entertaining** and perhaps also gently mocking or teasing, but they will not expect you to be:

✗ *overly sentimental*
✗ *revealing humiliating stories about the groom*
✗ *embarrassing or disrespectful to the bride*
✗ *dropping any kind of bombshell.*

Top tip
Yours is usually expected to be the longest of the speeches, but don't use this as an excuse to be long-winded. Make every word count.

● Don't drop any bombshells!

Representing others

If your speech only represents you in isolation, it is in danger of being introspective and private. Try instead to ensure that you represent **everyone present** by speaking in **open** and **inclusive** terms.

Pick the brains of other guests when compiling your material. This will help to ensure that your speech:

* has a **broad** appeal
* is **relevant** to as many people as possible
* has **variety**
* is **not cliquey**.

When using material (anecdotes, quotes, jokes, etc.) supplied by someone else, make sure you acknowledge it by saying something like:

* 'Someone was telling me that…'
* 'As some of you know…'
* 'Many of you will be familiar with…'

Pick the brains of other guests

Personalizing your speech

The last thing you want is to deliver a speech that could have been given by any best man, about any groom. **Every groom is different,** and so is every best man – so use this to your advantage. Guests may:

1 know the groom very well
2 know the groom somewhat
3 not know the groom.

This gives you the perfect opportunity to vary your speech to accommodate everyone, while making it personal to the groom. Depicting some of his more interesting character traits will ensure that your audience is:

Remember
Your speech should be personal and come from your feelings and memories, but done with a light touch and a sense of humour.

* amused to recollect his personality
* amused to learn something new about him
* amused to be introduced to him through his quirks!

3 Writing your speech: advanced techniques

The icing on the cake

To give your speech the **extra sparkle** that will elevate it above and beyond the majority of speeches and make it truly memorable, you will need to employ some more **advanced** speech-writing techniques. These will enable you to change a good speech into **a great speech.**

Through a process of **enhancements** and **fine tuning**, you will lift your speech to the next level. However, you will also need to be careful to negotiate any potential controversy or faux pas.

● Be prepared to go through a number of drafts to get to that great speech!

A great speech does not have to be complicated, but to be really successful it should **amuse** and **fascinate** your audience. You want such an important part of the wedding celebration to be recalled fondly for a long time afterwards.

This chapter focuses on the following advanced techniques:

* fine tuning
* keeping it focused
* appropriate humour
* avoiding humiliating references
* using anecdotes
* injecting variety
* avoiding controversy and faux pas
* dealing with awkward set-ups.

Change a good speech into a great speech

Fine tuning

Be prepared to revise your speech often, **crafting** it until you've **smoothed** off all the rough edges and removed any waffle. Try to get into the habit of **updating** it on a **regular** basis, particularly:

* after presenting it to anyone who is helping you practise
* after adding new material (check for repetition)
* after not looking at it for a few days (to gain perspective).

At the very least you should aim to revise your speech **once a week.** Consult the other speech givers too, to make sure that you are not repeating anything they have planned to say.

Remember
Great speeches aren't written; they're rewritten!

'If you can't write your message in a sentence, you can't say it in an hour.'
Dianna Booher

Keeping it focused

By ensuring that your material is first rate, you can reduce the need for fantastic comic delivery. Having a specific subject matter – the groom – is both a **help** and a **hindrance**.

Help

* It keeps your speech focused.
* You know exactly where to go for source material.
* People who know the groom will readily buy into your jokes.
* Everyone will be very much on your side.

Hindrance

* Your subject matter is limited.
* Your jokes and anecdotes must be based in truth.
* You have to be careful not to cause offence.

Top tip
Use this limitation as an opportunity to keep your speech **focused** and **relevant**.

Appropriate humour

Your speech will probably be the most eagerly anticipated of all the speeches. However, the audience may well feel apprehensive about the content.

You will need to ensure that your speech is:

✔ *appropriate for the entire audience*
✔ *appropriate to the occasion*
✔ *what the bride and groom would want.*

At the same time you will need to be sure that your material is not:

✘ *crass or lewd*
✘ *vulgar or offensive*
✘ *sexual in nature.*

Keep it clean!

Go through your speech and remove any **unsuitable** or **inappropriate** material – and use this on the **stag night** instead. By doing this you will:

✳ ensure it's not wasted
✳ have a great opportunity to practise delivering a speech to an audience
✳ get it out of your system!

Bullet Guide: The Fast Way to a Perfect Best Man's Speech

If it's humiliating it's not funny

It might be fun for you to ridicule the groom, especially if he's an old mate, and it may be fun for him too, but your speech needs to be enjoyable for everyone.

✔ **Do** consider whether the audience will find it **funny**, especially:
» the groom
» the bride
» their families
✔ Do know where to **draw the line!**

✗ Don't keep any **undesirable** material, no matter how funny it is
✗ Don't forget you're in **mixed company**
✗ Don't be tempted to **cross the line!**

Remember
Your audience will expect you to rib the groom but not to ridicule him. If the humour strays into cruelty it ceases to be funny.

Using anecdotes

This can be a great way to **introduce the groom** to guests who may not know him well – or even at all.

Using an anecdote allows you to convey:

* something of his **character**
* an **insight** into his personality
* interesting **background** information.

Crucially, using anecdotes means that this can all be achieved in a way that is:

* fun
* entertaining
* accessible.

Most of the wedding guests will know either the bride or groom but not necessarily both of them.

Top tip
A great way to get the audience on your side and help you relax is to relate an anecdote **about yourself and the groom.**

Injecting variety

Yours will typically be one of three speeches, so it's a good idea to inject some **variety** into it. To support and embellish your speech, you could:

* use **props**
* show **slides**
* play **music**.

Adding variety helps keep your speech fresh and will differentiate it from the other speeches. It also:

* creates **interest** for those listening
* **breaks up** your speech
* **divides** your speech into sections.

Top tip
Be careful not to overdo it! If your entire speech is filled with props, slides and music then this becomes the norm and ceases to add variety.

Adding variety helps keep your speech fresh

Avoiding controversy and faux pas

To ensure that the day **runs smoothly**, it's essential to avoid any faux pas. Crucial to this is **thorough research**. By learning as much as you can about the happy couple and their families, and any relevant sensibilities, you're well placed to avoid any subject areas that may be sensitive to them.

Try to make sure you:

✔ understand the **relationship complexities** of all parties
✔ ensure that your speech is **tactful** and **diplomatic**
✔ err on the side of **caution**
✘ omit any material you're **not sure** about
✘ are not tempted to **improvise**
✘ don't take **unnecessary risks**.

> **Remember**
> The groom chose you to be best man, so repay the compliment by showing him in a good light. Gentle ribbing only!

Dealing with awkward set-ups

Challenging family set-ups must be handled with tact and diplomacy.
First, identify any potentially awkward scenarios.

Absent family or friends might be:	You or your bride might have:
deceased	children
military personnel serving overseas	been married previously
in prison.	been previously engaged to one of the guests.

Any awkwardness can be overcome by
using the REDS acronym:

1 **R**esearch – what's the situation?
2 **E**nquiry – how would interested parties
   like the situation to be handled?
3 **D**etermine your course of action.
4 **S**tick to it.

● Be prepared to play piggy in the middle

4 Practising your speech

Practice makes perfect

We all know that 'practice makes perfect' and, if you're unused to **public speaking**, it's especially important to familiarize yourself with your speech and its delivery. By **practising** your speech, you will grow in **confidence** while honing your **technique** to ensure that you make the most of the occasion.

Don't feel you need to wait until your speech is written completely before you start practising – the sooner you start, the better!

The sooner you start, the better

When rehearsing your speech, think about what you are saying and how you would like to say it, and consider your **posture** and **body language** too. You can use a range of techniques to help you; this chapter explains how to:

* memorize your key points
* find your style
* make the mirror your best friend
* learn to stand still
* say it out loud
* rehearse in front of other people
* project the best 'you'
* exude confidence.

● Practise, practise, practise… anywhere, any time!

Memorizing your key points

Good speech delivery is a skill that needs to be learned and practised. The aim is not to be able to repeat the words verbatim, but to learn the content thoroughly enough to be able to memorize your key points. This will help you sound natural and feel relaxed while delivering your speech.

The amount of practice you'll need to put in will depend on a number of factors, including your:

* previous **experience**
* natural **aptitude**
* level of **confidence**.

Remember
Repetition through practice will not only improve your delivery but also help you control your nerves.

However, no matter what your starting position, the more practice you put in the better your speech will be. So practise **early** and practise **often**.

Finding your style

Use your preparation time as an opportunity to try out different ways of delivering your speech. When you find the **style** that **suits** you best, keep practising to refine and improve your delivery. A good way to edit your delivery is to record yourself delivering your speech.

As the saying goes, the more you put in the more you get out. As you become familiar with your speech, your confidence level will increase proportionately. As you gain in confidence, you will:

* start to feel more **relaxed**
* **slow down** your delivery
* begin to **enjoy** giving your speech.

By Jove, I think I've got it!

'It usually takes me more than three weeks to prepare a good impromptu speech.'

Mark Twain

Making the mirror your best friend

Practise your speech standing in front of **a full-length mirror.** Do you:

1 shuffle your feet?
2 fidget?
3 feel self-conscious?

By watching yourself, you can see and help to **eradicate any distracting habits** while building your confidence.

● The mirror can be a vital tool for self-presentation… and calming those nerves!

'How things look on the outside of us depends on how things are on the inside of us.'

Park Cousins

Top tip
Check your body language for potentially off-putting tics or mannerisms.

Learning to stand still

One of the most obvious **giveaways** of a **nervous speaker** or an under-rehearsed speech is someone **shuffling their feet.** Most people who do this (and that's most people!) don't even realize they're doing it.

To see if it applies to you, practise in front of:

1 a mirror   2 an invited audience.

If you shuffle, try imagining:	This will help you:
your feet are pinned to the floor	keep your feet firmly planted
a piece of string attached to the top of your head pulling you up.	keep yourself centred.

The result will be that you will stand still, which will help to:

* keep everyone **focused**
* make you look **confident**
* improve your **posture**
* enhance your **delivery**.

Saying it out loud

Most people are rarely conscious of hearing their own voice in everyday situations, but when it's the only sound in the room and everyone is listening to you, you'll hear it in a **whole new way**. It's something you'll have to get used to, so you'll need to practise saying your speech out loud.

Get used to hearing yourself

If you're not used to public speaking, you'll be amazed how odd your voice sounds at first. Try speaking out loud whenever you're on your own. This will:

* force you to **concentrate** on your voice
* give you an **opportunity** to get used to hearing yourself
* allow you to **experiment** with pace, pitch and tone
* make it seem **normal**!

Top tip
Try the vocal warm-up exercises in chapter 6 before saying your speech out loud.

Rehearsing in front of other people

'All the real work is done in the rehearsal period.'

Donald Pleasence

Practising your speech in front of an audience is **vital preparation** for the big day. You can start with just one person and build up to a few family members or close friends. Initially, you may feel:

* nervous
* awkward
* embarrassed
* self-conscious.

These feelings are entirely natural, but they will subside with practice and experience, leaving you free to enjoy giving your speech. It's far better to get over this hurdle now than face it for the first time on the big day.

Top tip
The more you practise, the easier it gets.

Projecting the best 'you'

When you stand up to make your speech, your guests become your audience. What is the **first impression** you want them to have of you?

✘ Nervous

✘ Dreading having to give your speech

✘ Worried you're going to make a fool of yourself

✘ Can't wait to get it over with.

✔ Confident

✔ In control

✔ Pleased to be there

✔ Looking forward to giving your speech.

The truth is that, no matter how you feel inside, your audience will only perceive what you **project** to them.

Remember
A swan may be paddling furiously below the water, but if on the surface it appears perfectly calm and composed no one will know.

Learning to exude confidence

Feeling confident is great, but you need to **exude** that confidence so that your audience will:

✳ feel in **safe hands**
✳ **relax**
✳ be free to **concentrate** on what you're saying.

'It's not who you are that holds you back, it's who you think you're not.'

Anon.

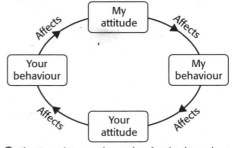

● The Betari Box – the cycle of attitude and behaviour

Remember
How you make your audience feel will directly affect how they make you feel, as the diagram shows.

5 Getting ready for the big day

Things to do in advance

It's vital to get yourself suitably **prepared** for the big day well in **advance**, both **practically** and **psychologically**. By doing so, you will leave yourself free to enjoy the wedding day to the full.

Nearer the time, it will help you relax if you have familiarized yourself with the **venue**, the **set-up** and the **practicalities** of your speech giving. Then there will be nothing to stop you delivering your speech to the best of your abilities.

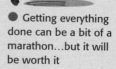

● Getting everything done can be a bit of a marathon…but it will be worth it

It's a good idea to make a **list** of the things you should do well before the day itself. This chapter offers useful tips on:

* checking out the venue
* practising your speech *in situ*
* using a microphone
* making cue cards
* preparing props.

This chapter also gives you **strategies** for how to overcome **unexpected** situations. Unforeseen scenarios have the potential to ruin your speech (or worse), so consider these possibilities and make plans for dealing with them.

Enjoy the wedding day to the full

Checking out the venue

The excitement of the day, and its significance and importance, will provide quite enough pressure without adding an unnecessary element of surprise. This is why it's essential to know exactly where you will be giving your speech.

Try to visit the wedding venue at least once before the day itself, to **familiarize** yourself with the room in which you'll be giving your speech. When you get there, take note of:

1 **where you'll be standing** to give your speech
2 **the size of the room**
3 the **acoustics** of the room
4 the **location** and **orientation** of the audience.

> **Top tip**
> Try to visit the venue when it's not busy so that you have the place to yourself to practise your speech.

* Find out whether you will just have to stand up and speak from your place at the table or whether you will have to walk to a pre-arranged spot. If it's the latter:
  » make sure you know how the groom finishes his speech, so you can be ready for a smooth **handover**
  » determine the **distance** you'll need to cover so you're there in good time
  » identify potential obstacles.
* If you're using props or giving gifts, find a suitable place to store them.

> The 'walk to the stage' can be the most awkward moment of the whole event. Everyone's eyes will be on you and the room may fall silent. Hold your nerve and look and act confident! Think of yourself as playing a part.

Practising your speech *in situ*

Nothing beats the experience of practising your speech **in the actual venue** in which the reception will be held. This will do wonders for your **confidence**, knowing that:

* it won't be a surprise on the day
* having done it once you can do it again
* next time you'll be surrounded by encouraging friends.

If you can repeat this on several occasions, you'll begin to concentrate on:

✔ *what you're saying*
✔ *how you're saying it*
✔ *how it's coming across*
✗ *rather than focusing on how you feel.*

Top tip
Take someone with you to provide an audience. This will add **realism** and provide an opportunity for feedback and checking sound levels.

Using a microphone effectively

Even if you feel you don't need one because you have a loud voice, unless the venue is **really intimate** it's usually best to use a microphone. This will:

1 take the **pressure off** you having to project
2 make you sound more relaxed, confident and **in control**
3 allow more **vocal expression** and subtlety
4 allow you to continue over any interruptions.

How to hold it	Where to hold it	How to speak into it
In a comfortable open fist, making sure you don't obscure the mesh	With the top of the microphone just in front of your chin	Speaking normally, keeping your voice at a constant volume

It's often best to use a microphone

Making cue cards

While it's obviously a good idea to become as familiar with your speech as possible, learning it by rote and delivering it without notes is **a recipe for disaster.** Pressure can make even the surest memory go blank.

Instead, write **brief notes on cue cards** to prompt you. It's best to…

* start each new thought on a separate line
* use smart, blank cards with plain backs.

Choose cards…

* small enough to fit comfortably in your hand
* big enough for writing you can read easily.

'Keep your words soft and tender because tomorrow you may have to eat them.'

Anon.

● Cue cards will prompt you for each part of your speech

Preparing props and slides

If you've decided to liven up your speech with props or audio-visual elements, it's best to prepare these as soon as possible. Doing so will give you time to:

✔ *practise with them*
✔ *make sure you know how they all work*
✔ *work them seamlessly into your delivery*
✔ *make sure you can get everything you need.*

If you're using technical items (such as sound, lighting or slides), check that:

☐ there will be a **power outlet** to hand
☐ you know how long they take **to warm up**
☐ you have a **back-up plan** if they fail to work.

Top tip
Using additional and unexpected elements to complement your speech can provide an extra dimension and add variety.

Unexpected problems

It might sound negative to try to imagine everything that could possibly go wrong, but it's worth it to **pre-empt problems**.

* Think through the whole of your speech, from the moment you place any props or presents to the moment you sit down after a job well done.
* Look at each moment and **envisage** as many different **challenging scenarios** as possible, and don't be afraid to think **outside the box**…

> Prevention is better than cure.

CASE STUDY: Expecting the unexpected

'One best man I know decided to use a projector to show photos of the groom as a baby – and it simply refused to work! Luckily he had printed sufficient copies, which were quickly distributed among the guests…'

Dealing with 'What if?' scenarios

Once you've identified the possible problems that might occur, think them through in turn and devise **a coping strategy** for dealing with each one. It also helps to think of **an alternative** in case the first is unsuccessful or insufficient.

What if...	Coping strategy	Last resort
...I lose my cue cards?	Keep a spare set (if possible already at the venue)	Make sure that another guest has an additional spare set
...someone persistently heckles?	Have a joke prepared to diffuse the situation	Ensure that you've primed someone to have a quiet word!
...I forget a key prop?	Have a spare already in place	Have prepared a way to communicate the idea without the prop

6 Dealing with nerves

The fear within

First things first: it's okay to be nervous. In fact, it's actually good to be nervous. Why? Because when you're nervous your body floods your system with adrenalin, which gives you an all-important **edge**. This edge will make you more alert and energetic, enabling you to deliver your speech with **power**, **passion** and **clarity**.

The trick is to learn to **harness** the adrenalin and use it to your advantage when you deliver your speech.

● We all get nervous…but learn to use those nerves!

This chapter explains why it's normal to be nervous before a public performance, and how to accept this as **nature's way** of getting you ready for the task ahead. It offers tips for using your pre-speech nerves to your advantage, and also tells you about:

* why it's important to release tension
* simple relaxation techniques
* confidence 'tricks of the trade'
* the importance of a good warm-up
* two-minute warm-ups that you can do anywhere.

It's okay to be nervous

Why it's good to be nervous

Everyone gets nervous before they have to speak in public. Not only is it perfectly natural, but it's also necessary. Your body is preparing you for a performance that you know is important.

Symptoms you might experience

☐ Heart racing
☐ Wobbly legs
☐ 'Butterflies' in the stomach
☐ Sweating
☐ Shaking hands
☐ Dry mouth
☐ Nausea
☐ Loss of appetite

How these can help you

* Nervousness releases adrenalin into your system, providing you with energy.
* Your body is being supercharged, ready to give a great performance.

Remember

Being nervous is good, but looking nervous isn't, so use the relaxation techniques described in this chapter to help overcome this.

Channelling your adrenalin

Take these steps to make your nervous energy
work for you:

✔ Practise your speech in front of
other people.
✔ Learn to recognize the feelings you
experience when you're nervous.
✔ Remind yourself that this is a good
thing.

> It's **your body** giving
> you an **edge**, heightening
> your **senses** and your **speed of
> thought** ready to deliver your
> speech to **maximum effect**.

> Tell me again
> why feeling this **bad**
> is a **good thing**?

PANIC

BUTTON

● No need to panic!

Why it's important to release tension

Even people who speak professionally experience nerves to some extent before giving a speech, so it's not surprising that most non-professional public speakers will feel some anxiety. It is important to try to relax, however, to rid your body – and your voice – of tension.

Tension in your body will:

* make you look nervous
* make you want to fidget
* impair your breathing.

Tension in your voice will:

* make you sound nervous
* make you sound strained
* make it difficult to control.

Being relaxed therefore **reduces your fear** and puts you in **control** of the situation.

'If nerves are a public speaker's best friend, tension is his worst enemy.'

David Windham

Simple relaxation techniques

The following exercises can be done individually or as a group.

Symptom	Exercise	Result
Tightness in shoulders	Shrug tightly, then relax. Repeat. Move shoulders in large circles	No visible tension
Tight voice	Yawn as widely as possible, and vocalize with an 'ahhh' sound	Voice does not sound strained
Shortness of breath	Breathe deeply, hold for ten seconds, breathe out and relax. Repeat	Sound relaxed and in control
Tightness in neck	Circle head slowly in a large arc, in both directions	Relaxed throat – improved vocal quality
Butterflies in stomach; general nervousness	Clench and relax different muscle groups in turn	Less nervousness
Clenched jaw	Swing jaw from side to side, first with mouth open, then closed	Relaxed jaw, allowing the sound out freely

Confidence tricks

Here are some 'tricks of the trade' that professional public speakers use to give them an air of confidence.

- ✔ Know your speech **thoroughly** – and **stick** to it
- ✔ Have a glass of **water** to hand
- ✘ Don't drink **alcohol** to calm your nerves – use the **relaxation techniques** instead
- ✔ Fight the temptation to **rush** your speech:
  - » speak slowly
  - » don't forget to pause
- ✔ Undo your **top button** (hidden behind cravat/tie)
- ✔ Pick out one person at a time and deliver that part of the speech directly to them
- ✔ Keep your **feet** still
- ✘ Don't speak over **laughter**

Top tip
Remember these tricks to appear calm, confident and relaxed – even if you're not.

Bullet Guide: The Fast Way to a Perfect Best Man's Speech

The importance of a good warm-up

Don't underestimate the importance of a thorough warm-up. Not only will it **relieve tension** and help you feel calm but it will also **prepare** you, **physically and mentally**, for the task ahead.

Warming up your body will:

* help you relax
* release pent-up adrenalin
* help prevent you shaking
* get rid of any 'wobbly' feelings
* put you in control.

Warming up your voice will:

* make it clearer
* allow everyone to hear you
* make you sound relaxed
* reduce hoarseness
* prevent strain.

A thorough warm-up will prepare you for the task ahead

Remember
Professional actors always warm up before a performance – and so should you.

Physical warm-ups

These two-minute exercises will help you to warm up your body, releasing tension in preparation for making your speech. You can perform them anywhere, very quickly – even in the Gents just before the speeches begin!

Deep breathing
1 Stand upright, relax your body and breathe in deeply.
2 Hold for ten seconds and slowly release.
3 Repeat five times.

Top tip
Use this time to think through your speech.

Stretching
1 Stretch up your arms as high as you can reach, standing on tiptoes.
2 Relax.
3 Stretch your arms as wide as you can.
4 Relax.
5 Repeat five times.

Scrunching and stretching your face
1 Scrunch up your face really tightly, pinching it in.
2 Relax.
3 Stretch your face as wide as possible, lifting your eyebrows and opening your mouth.
4 Relax.
5 Repeat five times.

Vocal warm-ups

These two-minute vocal exercises will help **release tension in your voice**. You can also perform them **anywhere**.

Yawning

1 Open your mouth wide and yawn loudly.
2 Repeat five times.

Humming

1 Hum one steady note, starting softly and growing louder.
2 Repeat, opening your mouth wide and allowing the sound out fully.
3 Repeat five times.

Lip and tongue mobility

1 Stick your tongue out and move it in large circles.
2 Repeat your favourite tongue twister.

● You can do your vocal warm-ups anywhere

7 Delivering your speech: the basics

An enjoyable performance

You've prepared your speech, and rehearsed it many times. You've got your cue cards ready and know the main points you are going to make. The only thing left to do is actually to make the speech.

There is **little point** in striving to **write** a **wonderful speech** and then **failing to deliver it well**. If it's not **enjoyable to listen to**, and your 'performance' isn't **enjoyable to watch**, your speech will be completely **undermined**.

On the other hand, everyone will love a well-delivered speech **given in an interesting way, with confidence**. It will be a **highlight** of the day and **remembered** for years to come.

This chapter covers the **basics of delivery**, including:

* putting your audience at ease
* setting the tone
* keeping to the script
* making eye contact
* avoiding fidgeting
* making sure you're heard
* the seven giveaways of a nervous speaker
* keeping the audience on your side.

A well-delivered speech will be a highlight of the day

● A happy audience

Putting your audience at ease

Everyone in the audience is willing you to do well, so avoid the temptation to tell them that you're not used to making speeches or that you're nervous, in the hope that it will:

* lower their expectations
* make you feel better
* break the ice.

It's a classic **trap** for the **unwary** and **inexperienced**, which instead will:

* make your audience uncomfortable
* make your audience nervous *for* you and *about* you
* undermine your speech.

Warning your guests that your speech won't be good is a great way to ensure that that's how they remember it – even if it was excellent. It's fine to be self-deprecating, as long as it doesn't detract from your purpose.

Setting the tone

Yours will be the last speech of the wedding, and you will want it to have a different **style** from the earlier speeches. It's therefore crucial to establish **the right tone** for your speech from **the outset.**

Your audience will probably be feeling:

✳ expectant
✳ excited
✳ nervous on your behalf.

You will therefore need to:

1 put them at ease – if they relax and are confident in your abilities it will help you relax and help them enjoy your speech

2 set an appropriate tone for the content of your speech, which might be:

» humorous   » cheeky
» irreverent   » friendly
» amused   » relaxed.

Top tip
Don't forget to introduce yourself at the start of your speech.

Keeping to the script

You've spent a lot of time and effort writing your speech – so stick to it! This will ensure that you:

✔ say **everything** you wanted to say
✔ keep your speech **tight** and **focused**
✔ look and sound **confident** and **in control**

✗ don't say anything you may later **regret**
✗ don't **dilute** your speech with poor material
✗ don't go on **too long**.

'No one ever complains about a speech being too short!'

Ira Hayes

● A successful speech giver sticks to the script

Making eye contact

Establishing and maintaining eye contact with the members of your audience will mean you see them as individuals rather than just a sea of faces. It's one of the most important aspects of good public speaking.

Eye contact allows you to:

* **engage** with your audience
* establish a **rapport** with them
* make each guest feel **included**
* **deliver** your speech with **dynamism**.

It will also help you to:

* look confident
* look interested
* feel less nervous
* keep your head up!

Top tip
Make eye contact with one guest at a time, starting with someone at the back of the room and delivering that part of your speech directly to them. Then move on to another guest.

Avoiding fidgeting

Any sort of fidgeting is both annoying to watch and distracting, and it will undermine what you're saying. Fidgeting is a natural reaction to being nervous and 'on show' but it must be avoided at all costs.

To prevent fidgeting, be aware of the ways in which you fidget – and the ways to combat them.

Type of fidgeting	Avoidance method
Shuffling feet	Keep feet firmly planted in one spot
Fiddling with rings or other jewellery	Keep hands on cue cards
Wringing hands	Keep hands apart
Running fingers through hair	Keep hands away from face and head
Shifting weight from one leg to the other	Keep weight centred
Rapid blinking	Concentrate on making eye contact

Making sure you're heard

There's no point in writing a great speech and mastering the subtleties of its delivery only to speak so quietly that you can't be heard. If you use a microphone, this will not be a problem; if not, you may be able to alter the mechanics of the venue to assist you. For example, you can:

* stand close to all the guests
* ensure that your audience is in front of you
* minimize background noise, by:
    » closing windows and doors
    » turning off air conditioning or heating.

In addition, to give yourself the best chance of being heard:

✔ speak loudly and evenly, and address the back of the room
✔ speak slowly and clearly

✔ keep your head up
✔ take a deep breath before each sentence.

Speak loudly and evenly

The seven giveaways of a nervous speaker

Controlling your nerves is important, but it's also important that you don't look nervous. Some of **the most common giveaways** you'll want to avoid are:

82

1 fidgeting
2 rapid swallowing
3 frequent coughing
4 nervous laughter
5 not lifting your head up
6 avoiding eye contact
7 speaking too quickly.

> **Remember**
> If you appear nervous, your audience will be nervous – which in turn will make you even more nervous! If you appear confident, your audience will relax – and so will you.

● How *not* to look!

Keeping the audience on your side

You have a great advantage here – your audience will comprise the happy couple's friends and family and they will be on your side from the outset. Your task, then, is to **keep them there!**

Five key tips

1 **Keep smiling** – even if you feel it's going badly.
2 **Make eye contact** with as many people as possible.
3 Don't be tempted to rush – **take your time** and let your audience enjoy your speech.
4 **Keep to the scrip**t – this will ensure that your material is first rate.
5 Try to **sound** as though you're enjoying yourself!

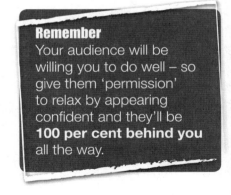

Remember
Your audience will be willing you to do well – so give them 'permission' to relax by appearing confident and they'll be **100 per cent behind you** all the way.

8 Delivering your speech: advanced techniques

An outstanding speech

Once you've got the hang of the basics of delivering your speech it's time to move on to the **more advanced techniques.** Mastering these can make all the difference between a delivery that is **competent** and one that is **outstanding.**

Such outstanding delivery will gain the **rapt attention** – and **admiration** – of **everyone** in the room. Your speech will be thoroughly enjoyed on the day and fondly remembered for a long time to come.

● Go the extra mile and your speech will fly!

It's possible to give a speech that will **enthral** your audience even if you have never spoken in public before. This chapter describes the skills and techniques you need to lift your speech to the **highest level**. It covers:

* dynamic delivery
* effective use of pauses and phrasing
* resisting the temptation to hurry
* overcoming mistakes
* varying your pace and pitch
* effective use of vocal tone and inflection.

Gain the rapt attention – and admiration – of everyone

Dynamic delivery

Dynamic delivery will hold your audience's attention and bring out the emotional responses you want. **Combining** the basic and advanced **techniques** for delivering your speech will enable you to present it in a manner that is:

* engaging
* sincere
* passionate
* inspirational
* memorable.

> **Top tip**
> Try out different combinations of techniques until you find your preferred style.

When you practise your speech, **experiment** with different techniques, preferably in front of people you can rely on for honest and constructive feedback. This will help you discover the combination of techniques that:

* best suits **your style**
* allows you to achieve the **desired tone**
* makes you feel most **comfortable**.

Using pauses and phrasing

Pauses help to **break up** the pattern of your speech so that it's pleasingly phrased. You want to avoid giving the impression that you are saying one long, never-ending sentence. Pauses will also:

1 allow your audience to **take in** what you've said
2 give your audience time to **laugh** – or to **reflect**
3 build **expectation**
4 **break up** a long story
5 **prevent** you from gabbling
6 allow you to **prepare** for the next part of your speech.

Top tip
If you wish to inject humour into your speech, try using a 'pregnant pause' – pausing at the end of a phrase to build suspense before a punch line.

'The most precious things in speech are pauses.'
Ralph Richardson

Resisting the temptation to hurry

If you're unused to public speaking, it's a natural to be tempted to rush your speech. This is almost always the result of nerves and the pressure of the occasion. However, try to avoid it because rushing:

* makes you sound **nervous**
* makes it difficult for the audience to **hear you**
* makes it difficult for the audience to **keep up.**

Just before you stand up to start speaking (and not too obviously), let out several deep, slow, controlled sighs to **fill your lungs** completely **with air.** This will help you to:

* start with a **good strong voice**
* maintain a **consistent flow of air**
* slow down your **heart rate**
* **distract** yourself from being nervous.

Top tip
Write the word
'pause' at intervals
through your notes
or cue cards.

Overcoming mistakes

During the course of your speech it's highly likely that you will make a mistake (or several!), especially if you are unused to public speaking. Mistakes in themselves don't matter; what matters is how you deal with them.

Common mistakes	How to overcome them
Stumbling over words	Just repeat them, more slowly
Losing your place in the 'script'	Take your time to find it again
Never lifting your head	Make regular eye contact
Speaking too quietly	Deliver every word to the back of the room
Panicking	Take a deep breath and carry on

'If you're not making mistakes, then you're not doing anything. I'm positive that a doer makes mistakes.'

John Wooden

Varying pace and pitch

The most interesting speech soon loses its appeal if delivered in a monotone. Varying pace and pitch provides **dramatic effect** and **emphasis**, helping to maintain your audience's interest.

Pace

Varying the pace of your delivery also helps you **underline** what you are saying.

Remember
Whatever pace you're aiming for, **go more slowly than you think you should.** Halve the speed you think feels right, and halve it again if you're nervous.

Speak **slowly** when you:

* are saying something serious
* need to be solemn
* want to add extra gravity to your message.

Speak **more quickly** when you:

* want to keep your message light-hearted
* are using humour
* are saying something upbeat.

Pitch

Another way to help convey your message is to **vary the pitch** of your voice according to the **content** of your speech and the **effect** you are hoping to have.

Use a **low** pitch to help convey:

* seriousness
* solemnity
* genuineness.

Use a **high** pitch to help convey:

* lightness
* humour
* joy.

Remember
The exact pitch of your voice will depend on whether your voice is naturally deep (low pitch) or naturally light (high pitch). Being aware of this will help to prevent you from delivering your speech with an unwanted vocal message!

Effective use of tone

Your tone of voice imparts the **underlying message** implicit in what you're saying, regardless of the content. Be aware of your tone since it can convey an **unwanted** or **unintended** sentiment.

By using tone, you can colour your voice with emotion or feelings, such as:

Don't talk to me in that tone of voice!

* happiness
* sadness
* pride
* warmth
* joy.

This will enable you to **convey** your feelings **quickly** and **openly,** and actively **support** your message.

Top tip
Before you deliver each part of your speech, think of an occasion when you felt the emotion you wish to convey.

Effective use of inflection

The inflection in your voice means the **rising** and **falling** patterns you create in your speech. Using inflection is important because it will:

* help paint a picture of what you're saying
* introduce vocal variety
* keep your audience interested
* underline the most important parts.

Top tip
Avoid the dreaded 'rising inflection'! Unless you are asking or posing a question, always make sure that you bring your voice *down* at the end of a sentence.

By **modulating** your voice, you can help to make your manner of speaking interesting to listen to, and deliver the content of your speech with maximum impact.

Make your manner of speaking interesting

9 Pitfalls and pratfalls – and how to avoid them

Potential hazards

Unless public speaking is your profession, you're likely to encounter a number of **unfamiliar situations** on the big day. Even when you have practised and prepared in order to give yourself the best possible **chance** of everything going smoothly, you will still be susceptible to **potential hazards** ready to wrongfoot the unwary.

'Forewarned is forearmed': by getting to know these pitfalls and pratfalls now, you can **plan** for all **eventualities**.

● Be on guard for 'banana skin' moments!

You want to make a speech of which you can be **proud**, free of blunders that might irritate or offend your audience. Likewise, you want to remain **unfazed** if something unforeseen happens during your speech. This chapter tells you how to avoid the most **common pitfa**lls, which are:

* trying to ad-lib
* allowing interruptions
* straying from the subject
* becoming overwhelmed
* using too many props
* relying on technology
* inappropriate material.

Forewarned is forearmed

Trying to ad-lib

Ad-libbing – making unscripted remarks **off the cuff** – is a skill best left to the professionals. They make it look easy, but don't be fooled: it's an incredibly difficult art to master and you're almost always better off **sticking to the script.** If your ad-lib is not brilliant, it can all too easily fall flat.

The biggest danger with ad-libbing is that, in the heat of the moment, under the pressure to perform and filled with adrenalin, you may **say something you wish you hadn't.**

You're better off sticking to the script

Remember
It only takes an unguarded second to say the wrong thing, but you might regret it for a long time.

Allowing interruptions

Friendly heckling during wedding speeches is common. Usually it's because:

* the heckler is nervous:
  * » for you
  * » for themselves (if they are speaking next)
* the heckler thinks it will help you by:
  * » providing a friendly voice
  * » drawing focus
  * » adding to your speech.

● Uncontrolled heckling can sabotage your speech

Top tip
Beware the snowball effect! If you allow one person to interrupt your speech, others might quickly jump on the bandwagon and, before you know it, you have been made redundant and left looking awkward.

Straying from the subject

If you have carefully written your speech and spent time practising and honing it, you are far better off keeping to it. Wandering off at a tangent will at best:

* **dilute** the content of your speech
* lose the **focus** of your message
* make you seem **less competent**.

At worst it will:

* have **little** or **nothing** to do with the **wedding**
* appear **selfish** and **rude**
* make your speech **unreasonably long**.

By sticking to the subject, you will:

* **know** what you're saying
* appear **confident**
* be in **control**.

● 'Will it never end?'

102

Becoming overwhelmed

Despite diligent practice and preparation, you won't be able to replicate exactly what it will be like on the day because of:

* the attendant **emotions** you'll experience
* the size of the **gathering**
* the **atmosphere** and sense of occasion.

If you start to feel overwhelmed:

* take several **deep breaths** first
* have a **glass of water** to hand, which will keep your mouth from drying and give you time to compose yourself.

Top tip
Avoid drinking alcohol to calm your nerves – it doesn't work and leaves you less in control.

'Confidence is preparation. Everything else is beyond your control.'

Richard Kline

Using too many props

While a good way to add variety to your speech is to use props, beware of using too many.

Props can be used to great effect to:	However, too many props can:
add humour	make your speech **cluttered**
create drama	**slow** you down
invoke nostalgia.	**draw emphasis** from what you're saying.

Props should therefore be kept to a minimum and used sparingly. Only include them if they are:

1 completely relevant
2 entirely appropriate
3 suitable to the occasion and the venue
4 going to complement your speech – not undermine it.

Top tip
Check out the venue in advance to determine where to keep props until you need them.

Bullet Guide: The Fast Way to a Perfect Best Man's Speech

Relying on technology

You may wish to employ some form of **technology** in your speech to add variety, create intrigue or just to give you a break. Some common examples are:

* **audio** recordings (for example, the groom singing in his first band)
* **video** recordings
* **slide** presentations.

However, all technology is susceptible to Murphy's Law: 'If it can go wrong, it will go wrong'! So always make sure you have a back-up plan.

Technology must be:

* relevant
* audible/visible to everyone
* ready to start and finish instantly.

Technology must not be:

* the mainstay of your speech
* generic (for example, copied straight from the internet)
* relied upon!

Inappropriate material

Your speech can quickly go horribly wrong if you include anything inappropriate. This can be material that is:

* risqué or lewd
* overtly political or radical
* likely to cause offence to specific guests.

Your wedding speech is not a time to take risks. **Err on the side of caution** and, if you're unsure about including something, leave it out. In particular, don't use this as an opportunity to:

* score points or gloat
* tell embarrassing stories
* mention exes
* use foul or abusive language.

'The real art of conversation is...to leave unsaid the wrong thing at the tempting moment.'

Dorothy Nevill

Suitable material

One of the challenges of giving the best man's speech lies in the **expectation** that you will **be funny.** However, it's all too easy to fall into the trap of using material that isn't really suitable or relevant just for the sake of getting a good laugh.

* Used **appropriately**, jokes…
  » are great time-fillers
  » keep everyone entertained
  » help to dispel your nerves.

Top tip
Use jokes **wisely** and **sparingly.**

However, jokes used **inappropriately** or too **liberally** will stick out like a sore thumb, no matter how funny they may be. Keep to the subject and vary your material to:

* keep the audience's **interest**
* make your delivery **lively**
* remain **relevant.**

10 Useful resources

Borrowing material

Your speech should be **unique** and **personal** to you and the happy couple, but that doesn't mean you shouldn't **borrow material** to supplement yours. After all, with the wit and wisdom of so many famous best men on which to draw, you're bound to find something that encapsulates exactly what you want to say, and says it superbly.

And, thanks to the **internet**, research has never been easier.

● A pithy, witty quote can be a brilliant resource

There is a treasury of possible material that you could include in your speech. Make sure you choose something **suitable** for your particular circumstances and that you know will **appeal** to your audience.

In this chapter you'll find just a **tiny selection** of the vast range of sayings, witty words and other material you can borrow to spice up your speech, including:

* humorous and witty quotes
* words of wisdom
* jokes
* toasts
* poems.

Thanks to the internet, research has never been easier

Humorous quotes

A good quote can provide an **excellent route into your speech,** as well as providing some great **comic material** quickly. For example:

'A man in love is incomplete until he is married. Then he's finished.'
Zsa Zsa Gabor

'I love being married. It's so great to find that one special person you want to annoy for the rest of your life.'
Rita Rudner

'They have come up with a perfect understanding. He won't try to run her life, and he won't try to run his, either.'
Anon.

'Marriage – a book of which the first chapter is written in poetry and the remaining chapters written in prose.'
Beverly Nichols

'You have to kiss a lot of toads before you find a handsome prince.'
Anon.

'Marriage is a wonderful invention:
then again, so is a
bicycle repair kit.'
Billy Connolly

'Marriage is a wonderful
institution ... but who wants
to live in an institution?'
Groucho Marx

'Bigamy is having one wife too
many. Monogamy is the same.'
Oscar Wilde

'It's a funny thing that
when a man hasn't anything
on earth to worry about,
he goes off and gets married.'
Robert Frost

'Marriage means commitment.
Of course, so does insanity.'
Anon.

'He early on let her know
who is the boss.
He looked her straight in the eye
and said clearly,
"You're the boss."'
Anon.

'Marriage is when a man
and woman become as one;
the trouble starts when they
try to decide which one.'
Anon.

Witty quotes

'The proper basis for a marriage is mutual misunderstanding.'
Oscar Wilde

'The woman cries before the wedding; the man afterwards.'
Anon.

(Follow this one up by looking closely at the groom and saying, 'He seems to be holding it together so far but it's only a matter of time!')

'I always cry at weddings, especially my own.'
Humphrey Bogart

'Marriage is like a hot bath. Once you get used to it, it's not so hot.'
Anon.

'Behind every great man there is a surprised woman.'
Maryon Pearson

'Marriage is like a violin. After the music is over, you still have the strings.'
Anon.

'Marriage is an adventure, like going to war.'
G.K. Chesterton

'I don't worry about terrorism.
I was married for two years.'
Sam Kinison

'Bride, n. A woman with
a fine prospect behind her.'
Ambrose Bierce

'Marriage is the triumph of
imagination over intelligence.
Second marriage is the triumph
of hope over experience.'
Oscar Wilde

'Marriage is the process
of finding out what kind of person
your spouse would have
really preferred.'
Jay Trachman

'Marriage is not a word;
it is a sentence.'
King Vidor

'Marriage is a mutual relationship
if both parties know when
to be mute.'
Anon.

'The most dangerous food is
wedding cake.'
American proverb

'The secret of a happy marriage
remains a secret.'
Henny Youngman

Words of wisdom

'Compromise:
An amiable arrangement
between husband and wife
whereby they agree to let her
have her own way.'

Anon.

'Marriage requires a person
to prepare four types of "rings":
Engagement ring, wedding ring,
suffering, enduring.'

Anon.

'Keep your eyes wide open before
marriage, half shut afterwards.'

Benjamin Franklin

'By all means marry.
If you get a good wife
you will become happy,
and if you get a bad one
you will become a philosopher.'

Socrates

'Both marriage and death
ought to be welcome:
The one promises happiness,
doubtless the other assures it.'

Mark Twain

'No man was ever shot by his wife
while doing the dishes.'

Anon.

Jokes

* 'Ladies and Gentlemen, if there's anyone here who's feeling, worried, nervous or apprehensive it's probably because you just married John.'
* 'Phil, you're a lucky man, marrying Jen today. She deserves a good husband...unfortunately you got to her before she had a chance to find one!'
* 'Rob has married a wonderful woman. I would say some other nice things about Amy, such as how bright she is, but that would be pushing it because she's just married Rob of her own free will.'

● Remember your audience – jokes must be funny but *never* smutty or embarrassing!

Toasts

Your toast should be sincere but that's no reason not to make its introduction humorous. Here are some examples:

* 'John, you are a lucky man; you've got Mary. She's beautiful, smart, funny, warm, and loving. And Mary, you've got – well, you've got…John.'
* 'Love is like a long and beautiful dream. Getting married is the wake-up call!'
* 'An ancient Chinese proverb reads: "He who holds hands before exchanging wedding vows is in love. He who holds hands afterwards is defending himself."'

> **Remember**
> Whatever toast you use, it should finish with a rousing 'Ladies and gentlemen, please join me in a toast to the bride and groom!'

Poems

Reading a poem is a great way to add variety to your speech. It will also give you a pause from directly addressing the audience. Examples include:

* 'Valentine' (Wendy Cope)
* 'I Wanna Be Yours' (John Cooper Clark)
* 'Oh the Places You'll Go' (Dr Seuss)
* 'Yes, I'll Marry You' (Pam Ayres)
* 'He Never Leaves the Seat Up' (Pam Ayres)
* 'I'll Be There for You' (Louise Cuddon)
* 'A Lovely Love Story' (Edward Monkton)
* 'I Rely On You' (Hovis Presley)
* 'I Wanna Be Yours' (John Cooper-Clarke)
* 'Recipe for Love' (Author unknown)
* 'I Wanna Grow Old With You' (Adam Sandler – song lyrics from the movie *The Wedding Singer*)
* 'Saga Love' (Bee Rawlinson)

Top tip
Don't choose a poem that's too emotional or 'profound' – this is a joyous occasion, not a literary salon!